# Ramprasad
## THE MELODIOUS MYSTIC

SWAMI BUDHANANDA

D1533118

# Advaita Ashrama
(Publication Department)
5 Dehi Entally Road
Kolkata 700 014

*Published by*
SWAMI MUMUKSHANANDA
PRESIDENT, ADVAITA ASHRAMA
MAYAVATI, CHAMPAWAT, HIMALAYAS
*through its Publication Department, Kolkata*
*Email: advaita@vsnl.com*
*Website: www.advaitaonline.com*

First published by Ramakrishna Mission,
New Delhi, in December 1982
Second edition, August 2002
3M3C


ISBN 81-7505-240-6

*Printed in India at*
Trio Process
Kolkata 700 014

# CONTENTS

## PUBLISHER'S NOTE TO THE FIRST EDITION

The more *The Gospel of Sri Ramakrishna* spreads in the world, the greater number of people ask: Who is this Ramprasad, whose songs Sri Ramakrishna so often sang?

This small book, *Ramprasad: The Melodious Mystic*, is designed to be a modest answer to the above question.

This short life of Ramprasad was first serialized in the *Vedanta Kesari*, an English Organ of the Ramakrishna Order, in its May through August 1959 issues.

After more than twenty years the writing is finding its way into the world of seekers in the form of this book, now enlivened by the sketches drawn by artist Biswaranjan Chakraborty, who has also drawn the elegant and eloquent cover design.

We do hope that by the grace of the Divine Mother this book will find ready entry into the seekers' hearts,

and they will enjoy reading it and passing it on to fellow
devotees.

12 December 1982                                    PUBLISHER
Ramakrishna Mission
New Delhi

# PREFACE

Sri Ramprasad (1723-1803), the melodious mystic of Bengal, belongs to that wonderful galaxy of Indian mystics whose approach to the Divine found expression and consummation in songs and melodies which form a part of the spiritual heritage of India. In this group are to be counted, among others, saints such as Tukaram, Namadev, Tulsidas, Mirabai, Surdas, Jayadev, Chandidas, Vidyapati of North India and Sri Purandaradas, Sri Tyagaraja, Shyama Sastri, Muthuswami Dikshitar and Ramalinga Swamigal of South India.

People of South India will be interested to know that Ramprasad was a senior contemporary of the celebrated three South Indian mystics—Sri Tyagaraja, Shyama Sastri, and Muthuswami Dikshitar. And it is not surprising that these melodious mystics sometimes sang alike, theirs being, after all, the same urge—the devotee's longing for the Deity, the finite's hunger for the Infinite, the soul's yearning for the Over-soul.

To the devotees of Sri Ramakrishna, Ramprasad has a special appeal, for the songs of Ramprasad, the Kali worshipper, were an abiding inspiration in Sri Ramakrishna's life. In the days of his sadhana, Sri Ramakrishna used to sing the songs of saints like Ramprasad before the image of the Divine Mother as a part of his daily worship. The readers of the *Gospel of Sri Ramakrishna* know how often the Master would rise to his feet singing a song of Ramprasad and go into samadhi. The language, mood, *bhava,* imagery and humour of Ramprasad's songs suited Sri Rama-krishna's spiritual temper so well that he remained a lifelong singer of Ramprasad's songs. On his lips these songs, which had been composed about a century earlier, became charged with an added spiritual power, incidentally revealing the author of those songs in the fullness of his glorious spiritual stature.

Ramprasad's life is not very widely known outside Bengal. It can be a great source of inspiration to all earnest sadhakas, especially worshippers of the Divine Mother. Hence, the knowledge of his life deserves to be propagated in all the languages of India.

For the material of this small book the writer has mainly depended on *Sadhak Ramprasad* by Swami Vamadevananda, in Bengali, published by Udbodhan Office, Kolkata.

The renderings of the songs of Ramprasad found asterisked are quoted from the *Gospel of Sri Ramakrishna,* translated by Swami Nikhilananda, published by Sri Ramakrishna Math, Chennai.

This small book is not claimed to be an exhaustive biography of Ramprasad. An attempt, however, has been made here to portray the inner moods, the beauty and grandeur of his soul. And I thankfully acknowledge that in this attempt Biswaranjan Chakraborty's sketches have significantly enriched and enlivened the publication.

7 December 1982                    Swami Budhananda
Holy Mother's Birthday

# Ramprasad
## THE MELODIOUS MYSTIC

# THE CULTURAL BACKGROUND
## AND EARLY LIFE

$\mathcal{K}$umarhatta (Kumarhati) is the name of the village in the district of 24 Parganas on the bank of the Ganga, 55 kilometres north of Kolkata. This village at one time excelled in learning and culture even Navadwip, a great seat of learning and the birthplace of Sri Chaitanya. An interesting story is told of how it came to have the name 'Kumarhatta'.

On one occasion a large number of scholars from Navadwip came to Halisahar (another name of Kumarhatta) with a view to challenge the local scholars to polemics on the scriptures *(shastra-vichara)*. But the scholars of Halisahar adopted a clever ruse to avoid the fateful discussion. They sent a young potter disguised as a woman to serve the visiting scholars. The woman accompanied by a young boy, posing as her son, managed to get herself appointed as the maid-

11

servant of the guests. Needless to say, this (potter) maidservant was duly tutored by the scholars of Halisahar before she was sent to her job.

Very early next morning the maidservant was found conscientiously busy with her household duties. As the day dawned, the crows began to caw. The young child of the maidservant ran to her and asked, 'Mother, mother, why do the crows caw?'

'How do I know that?' replied the mother. 'I am an ignorant woman. Go and ask those pundits who have come from Navadwip.'

The boy went to the scholars and repeated the question. 'How do we know that?' said the puzzled scholars, 'perhaps they are cawing because it is morning.'

Dissatisfied with the answer, the boy returned to his mother and demanded an immediate clarification of this momentous issue. This time the mother silenced the importunate child by reciting a Sanskrit couplet to say:

तिमिरारिस्तमो हन्ति शंकाकुलित मानसा: ।
वयं काका: वयं काका: इति जल्पन्ति वायसा: ॥

'The sun destroys darkness. Afraid that they too might be destroyed, being taken as part of the darkness, the crows shout out "we are crows, we are crows".'

Amazed to hear Sanskrit citations on the lips of the maidservant, the learned men asked her how she

The trick of Halisahar scholars

acquired this learning. 'I reside in the vicinity of scholars,' she replied, 'and the scholars are always discussing Sanskrit.' If a maidservant could be so learned, the clever pundits mused, it was foolish to face the scholars. And they decamped that very day.

The scholars of Halisahar were thus saved from a difficult situation. Out of gratitude to this potter, it is said, they named their village Kumarhatta—'Kumar' in Bengali meaning a potter, and 'hatta', a village market.

In this village, with a background of such scholarship and culture, Ramprasad was born, probably, in 1723, in a hereditary Tantric vaidya family. His father, Ramram Sen, was an eminent Ayurvedic physician and a Sanskrit scholar too. His mother, Siddheshwari, was the second wife of his father. By the first wife, Ramram Sen had one son, Nidhiram; and by the second wife, two daughters and two sons—Ambika, Bhavani, Ramprasad and Vishwanath.

As a little boy, Ramprasad was sent to the village school where he proved himself to be an extra-ordinarily meritorious student, finishing the entire course in a very short time. His father, reputed Ayurvedic physician that he was, naturally wanted his son to take up his own family profession in due course. Hence he sent him to a Sanskrit *tol*, where, in a short time, Ramprasad attained proficiency in *vyakarana* and *kavya*. But to the great disappointment of his father,

Ramprasad's aversion to professional learning

Ramprasad showed no interest in Ayurveda. Instead, he desired to learn some other languages. The wise father directed him to learn Persian and Hindi, thinking that the learning of these two languages might bring him opening in life, Bengal then being under Muslim rule.

## SPIRITUAL AWAKENING AND MARRIAGE

*F*rom about his eighteenth year, Ramprasad evinced that sort of indifference to the world, which is often thought to be a disease of the mind, curable only by the wonder-drug known as marriage. When he was twenty-two the anxious parents got him married to one Sarvani, by whom, in due course, he had four children—two daughters, Parameshwari and Jagadishwari, and two sons, Ramdulal and Rammohan.

According to the family tradition, the newly married couple were initiated by their family Guru just after their marriage. Though Ramprasad was married and was not insensitive to the attractions of his wife, a greater attraction, not always definite and defined, an agony—painful yet sweet—for the Divine had such a tremendous sway over his mind and aspirations that he could never discipline himself to the responsibilities which normally devolve on a householder. Rather, he

Ramprasad's other-worldliness causes anxiety
to his parents

devoted himself more and more to the practice of spiritual discipline.

But suddenly one day the family Guru passed away. An earnest seeker, however, is never left without proper guidance. As if brought by a divine directive, a great Tantric sadhaka and scholar, Agamavagisha by name, came to Kumarhatta. Attracted by his spirituality, people began to throng about him. One day Ramprasad met him alone in a solitary spot. At the first glance Agamavagisha saw Ramprasad to be an extraordinary man with a great spiritual future. Then followed a period of instruction in the intricacies of Tantric sadhana. After a time the Guru left and the disciple became absorbed in sadhana.

Agamavagisha divines Ramprasad's great
spiritual potential

## DIVINE INTIMATIONS
## AMIDST ENCIRCLING GLOOM

*R*amprasad's father, Ramram Sen, being himself a religious man, could not object to his son's earnestness about religious practices. But all the same, he, as a man of experience, could foresee how dark would be the future of the family when he died. And when actually he died all of a sudden, Ramprasad did find himself beset with an awful darkness. It was beyond his imagination how heavy could be the burden of a small family, until it actually fell heavily on his shoulders. The father had not left considerable patrimony. Ramprasad, though a scholar in *kavya, darshana*, Persian and Hindi, was perfectly innocent as to the ways of earning his livelihood and maintaining a family.

Could not the Mother of the Universe, whom he had all along been so devotedly worshipping, help him out now? With fervent hope, he continued to make his

intense supplications to the Mother. But afterwards
he knew better and sang with wonderful buoyancy:

> Mother, strange is the beauty
>> of one who becomes your devotee![1]
> He does not even get a piece
>> of cloth to adorn his loins!
> His body is smeared with ash
>> and he carries matted locks on his head.

Contrary to common notions, the Divine
Mother's grace comes to us in the form not only of
plenty, but in the form of destitution too. It is not
until one has learnt to regard destitution and misery
also as manifestations of Mother's grace, that one has
begun to love the Mother. In his great poem, 'Kali the
Mother', Swami Vivekananda heroically sang:

> Who dares misery love,
> And hug the form of death,
> Dance in destruction's dance,
> To him the Mother comes.

The much-prayed-for help did not appear to come
to Ramprasad from the Mother whom he worshipped.
At last, under the compulsion of circumstances, this
sadhaka-scholar wended his way to Kolkata. All the
time chanting the name of the Mother, this fugitive

---

[1] काली सब घुचालि लेटा।

from the world entered the city in search of the
wherewithal of life. Imagine this helpless man of God—
torn between the demands of the two worlds, one
exacting and the other elusive—knocking about at this
door and that for a job, but all the time anxious to run
away somewhere and drown himself in the depths of
sadhana!

Ultimately he got the job of a clerk in the house of
one Durgacharan Mitra of Garanhata, on a salary of
thirty rupees a month. And Ramprasad's gratitude to
the Divine Mother knew no bounds. Songs welled up
from the depth of his soul. In supreme love and
adoration, Ramprasad wrote:

O Mother! Give me your treasurer-ship,[2]
I am not ungrateful, O Shankari.
I cannot stand all and sundry
     looting the treasure of your feet.
Forgetful Tripurari is your steward—
Shiva is pleased with a trifle and is generous by nature,
Yet you keep your treasure under his charge.
Half the body is leased out,
     but what a heavy salary for Shiva.
I am your servant without pay,
My only right is to the dust of your feet.
If you adopt your father's way, then I stand defeated.

---

[2] आमায় दाओ मा तविलदारी।

If, however, you adopt my father's way,
> then I may attain you.
Says Prasad, I am undone with
> the trouble of such a post,
But if I can get at those feet of yours,
> I can easily get over my difficulties.

Songs like these and the name of the Mother were being written in the book meant for writing accounts! And what superior officer would put up with this sort of nonsense in an account book and with such a spoiler of accounts? In ecstasy, Ramprasad would just not remember what he was doing. Then the name and song of the Mother welled forth from the depths of his soul and he would write in poetic figures quite different from the figures of account books. And so other mistakes began to occur. No one expects, much less tolerates, mysticism in a mere clerk. Complaints were duly and dutifully carried to the master, who was not found to be very keen in apprehending the gravity of the lapses committed by the new employee. But the tenacity of the complainants ultimately got the better of the indulgent mood of the master, who, one day, out of sheer annoyance, sent for Ramprasad. The enthusiastic officer brought before the master both Ramprasad and the account book in which the inspired songs on the Mother had been written. The master began to scrutinize the account book thoroughly. As he came to the lines: 'I am your servant without pay.

I have only the right to the dust of your feet...,' tears rolled down from his eyes, to the great bewilderment of the complainant.

Now, regarding Ramprasad with great veneration and affection, the master uttered the following unexpected words:

> Ramprasad, you have not been born in this world just to eke out a humdrum existence. You wanted the treasurer-ship of the Mother. You will get it in the fullness of time. For the time being, return home and devote yourself to spiritual practices. Do not be sorry thinking that you have spoilt my account book. On the other hand, by the writings of your hallowed hand you have sanctified the account book, which will be kept in my family as a precious heirloom in order to give account of your devotion to the Divine Mother. Go home now. You will get an allowance of thirty rupees every month from my family.

On being brought before the master, Ramprasad was in an ecstatic mood, all the time chanting the name of the Mother. Now, when he heard these very noble words of the kind master, his high-charged emotions spontaneously broke forth in a song:

> O mind, ruinous fellow,[3]
> You do not know you are no beggar,

---

[3] मन তুइ কাঙ্গালী কিসে।

Ramprasad breaking into a song on hearing kind words
of his employer

You go about from country to
          country seeking transient treasure,
Whereas you can sit still and regard the immeasur-
          able treasure lying in your own house.
If you are genuine, O mind,
          be conscientious in yoga.
No poison will prove fatal to you,
When the state of involuntary
          Yoga will have been attained.
Take good care of the treasure-purse given by Guru.
This is humble Ramprasad's supplication
For the attainment of the fearless feet.

Immensely pleased to hear the song, the master
sent Ramprasad home rewarding him with a number
of presents.

Maharaja Krishnachandra's first rapport with
Ramprasad's songs

# BACK HOME IN SEARCH OF
# THE MOTHER DIVINE

*B*ack home, Ramprasad gave the good news to his mother to whom he was always greatly devoted. His mother made obeisance to the Mother of the Universe in her turn.

The spontaneous flow of Ramprasad's lyrical life, which had been arrested owing to the necessity of supporting a family, now resumed. Unobstructed and unworried, Ramprasad again got immersed in sadhana. His natural devotion now broke forth spontaneously in waves of song to the Divine Mother Kali.

One of his peculiar habits was to stand neck-deep in the Ganga and continue to sing loudly song after song in his powerful voice. These songs, surging up from the *hridaya-Ganga*[4] of Ramprasad, would mingle

---

[4] The Ganga of devotion flowing in his heart.

with the sweet murmur of the Ganga itself and fill the atmosphere drawing local people in numbers to the banks. While Ramprasad, absolutely lost in himself, went on singing, passengers in boats would stop near the banks just to listen to his soul-stirring songs. It is said that once, while cruising on the Ganga, Maharaja Krishnachandra of Navadwip was so charmed to hear Ramprasad's songs that he waited in his boat for a long time until Ramprasad had finished his devotions.

This Maharaja Krishnachandra, himself a talented man, was in his day a great patron of talent in that part of the country. Even as Vikramaditya's court was adorned by *navaratnas*,[5] among whom was the great Kalidasa, the immortal poet, so Maharaja Krishna-chandra's court was adorned by poet Bharatachandra, by the great Tantrik sadhaka, Agamavagisha, and by Gopal Bhand, the court jester.

Like a jeweller irresistibly attracted to a rare jewel, Krishnachandra respectfully approached Ramprasad and suggested that he too might come and adorn his court. What was the reaction of Ramprasad at this windfall which would solve material problems of his life for ever? Was Ramprasad beside himself with joy at this sudden stroke of good luck? No, he felt as though struck by a thunderbolt. How could one in

---

[5] Nine Gems, meaning nine luminaries.

whose heart the Mother of the Universe was enthroned think of becoming a courtier? Humbly and gracefully Ramprasad declined the offer of the Maharaja, who, in turn, grew all the more respectful at the blazing renunciation of this young aspirant.

One may recall here how, when Lakshminarayan Marwari offered to make an endowment of ten thousand rupees for personal expenses, Sri Ramakrishna fell unconscious as if struck on the head. Strange men these, who were mad with love of the Divine Mother! The values of the world were no values for them.

But Maharaja Krishnachandra was not to be easily put off. He persuaded Ramprasad to accept a gift of a hundred bighas of land free of rent as the hereditary right of his family.

The Divine promise in the *Gita* (ix. 22) was:

Persons who worship Me without any other thought, to them thus absorbed, I carry what they lack and preserve what they already have.

If the validity of this promise requires proof, here it is. Ramprasad had given his heart and soul to the Mother. Was it not then Mother's duty to look after this child who did not seek any other support in the world?

As a mark of gratitude for this act of kindness, Ramprasad afterwards presented to the Maharaja his poetical work 'Vidyasundar.'

It is also said that Nawab Sirajuddaullah was once

Ramprasad meets Nawab Sirajuddaullah

likewise charmed to hear Ramprasad's songs while afloat on the Ganga and invited the latter to accompany him to Murshidabad. Ramprasad could not accept the invitation immediately, but it is presumed that after some time he went once to Murshidabad in response to the Nawab's invitation.

With his wants removed by the grace of the Divine Mother, Ramprasad now went all out in his sadhana. Without staking one's all, without diving deep into sadhana, one will not get at the gems of realization. This mood took possession of Ramprasad and he spontaneously sang:

   \*Taking the name of Kali, dive deep down, O mind,[6]
    Into the heart's fathomless depths,
    Where many a precious gem lies hid.
    But never believe the bed of the ocean bare of gems
    If in the first few dives you fail;
    With firm resolve and self-control
    Dive deep and make your way to Mother Kali's realm.

    Down in the ocean's depths of heavenly Wisdom lie
    The wondrous pearls of Peace, O mind;
    And you yourself can gather them,
    If you have but pure love
       and follow the scriptures' rule.
    Within those ocean depths, as well,

---

[6] डुब देरे मन काली बोले।

3

Six alligators lurk—lust, anger and the rest—
Swimming about in search of prey.
Smear yourself with the turmeric of discrimination;
The very smell of it will shield you from their jaws.
Upon the ocean bed lie strewn
Unnumbered pearls and precious gems;
Plunge in, says Ramprasad,
        and gather up handfuls there!

Under the Panchavati[7] in a garden near his house,
he made a *panchamundi asana*[8] and engaged himself in
a most severe sort of sadhana, going home only twice
a day for food. On such days as *ekadashi, purnima* and
*amavasya,* he would not go home at all, being immersed
all the time in the worship and adoration of the Divine
Mother. Song after song surged forth in agonizing
supplication:

O Mother, shall I remain just like this....?[9]

I shall not call you Mother any more,[10]

---

[7] Comprising of Ashvatha, Vilva, Amalaki, Ashoka and Vata trees.
[8] In one method of spiritual discipline, according to Tantra
scriptures, the aspirant is required to practise meditation seated
on an altar inside which are interred five skulls, that of a snake,
frog, rabbit, fox and man. This altar is called a *Panchamundi asana,*
seat of five skulls.
[9] আমি কি এমনি রবো মা তারা।
[10] মা মা বোলে আর ডাকবোনা।

Ramprasad preparing the *panchamundi asana*

You have given and are giving me,
        no end of troubles...

Mother, how long you will make me go about[11]
Like a bull with blinkers on
Round and round the oil-press?

Tell me Mother, where do I stand?[12]
I have none here to call my own
O Shankari...

Ordinary mortals cannot imagine the sufferings of a sadhaka who has given up this world of din and dross, of dust and lust, but has not gained the other world of light and joy, of knowledge and bliss. He is at times in agony, in choking darkness.

---

[11] मा आमाय घोराबे कत।
[12] बोल मा तारा दाडाइ कोथा।

# VISIONS OF THE DIVINE MOTHER

The Divine Mother, one day, endowed his acute moments of agony bursting forth in the form of soul-rending supplications, and all his sadhanas, with meaning and value. It is said that Ramprasad had the first vision of the Mother in a garden near his house. As a result of it, even his physical appearance was transformed. At about that time a glow would radiate from his body. Everybody noticed it, but they did not know what was the cause of it.

After this vision of the Divine Mother, wonderful things happened in Ramprasad's life, things usually called 'miracles'. Once it came about that, owing to poverty caused by his unworldliness, he had to repair a hedge himself. His daughter, Jagadishwari, was helping him by returning the cord from the other side of the hedge. After some time Jagadishwari was called away. When she returned, she found that the work

Ramprasad being helped by the Divine Mother
Herself in repairing the fence

had gone on, and she asked with surprise who had been returning the cord all the time while she was away.

'Why, my child, you have been doing that all this time,' said Ramprasad, intrigued at the question.

'No, father, I was not here at all for a long time, having gone away on some other work.'

Then who had been returning the cord? For some time Ramprasad sat dumbfounded. Convinced that the Divine Mother Herself, in the form of his daughter, was all the time helping him in repairing the hedge, in gratitude he broke into a song:

> O mind, why do you keep
> > away from the Mother's feet?[13]
> O mind, meditate on the Mother,
> > you will get then mukti,
> Tie then (the Mother's feet)
> > with the cord of devotion.
> So bad is your luck that though having eyes,
> You did not see that the Mother came as your daughter
> And tied the hedge with the devotee.

On another occasion, when Ramprasad was about to go for a bath, an exceptionally beautiful young woman came and wanted to hear his songs. Asking her to wait, Ramprasad went for his bath. On returning

---

[13] मन केन मायेर चरणछाडা।

he searched for the lady, and she was not to be found anywhere. As his eyes fell on the wall of the temple hall, Ramprasad was surprised and thrilled to read the words:

> I am Annapurna, came to hear your songs, cannot wait any longer now. Go to Kashi and sing before Me.

The Mother Annapurna had Herself come! And to have turned her away for the sake of taking a bath! Torn with anguish and remorse, Ramprasad at once started for Kashi. But finally he had not to go that far. It is said that on the way, near Triveni, he was instructed in dream that it would be sufficient if he sang from there itself and that he had not to proceed further. Accordingly, seated near Triveni, in joy and gratitude, Ramprasad lost himself in singing song after song, which issued from the depth of his heart like a spring of limpid water. It was as if Saraswati herself, seated in his throat, was composing those songs.

Many stories like these are told about Ramprasad. But the authenticity of them all can no longer be ascertained. In any case, Ramprasad was now given unto Kali and indifferent to the world. Even so, he was attached to this mother, being himself a Mother-worshipper. But now, when his own mother died, the last string which had tied his mind to mundane things was severed. With his father's

Annapurna asks Ramprasad to sing to Her

Ramprasad doing the most severe sort of sadhana

death the crushing burden of the family had fallen on his head; with his mother's, awareness of that burden was wiped out.

It is at about this time that Ramprasad did the most severe sort of sadhana, sitting on a dead body in a cremation ground and being, in due course, blessed with the vision of Adyashakti Mahamaya.

With these realizations crowding in on him, Ramprasad's days would pass in ecstatic absorption in the Mother, whom he now perceived everywhere in the universe. Days and nights would pass without food and sleep while he was blissfully wakeful in yoga, in spontaneous and joyous communion with Mother.

Aju Gonsai-Ramprasad encounter

# RAMPRASAD AND AJU GONSAI

*W*ith Ramprasad is associated a strange person, who brings some colour and humour in an otherwise rigorous life of intense sadhana. One Aju Gonsai, a Vaishnava by faith, was a neighbour of Ramprasad. People knew him to be a crack-brained fellow, but he was gifted with some poetic talent and had a little scholarship too. He took delight in parodying Ramprasad's songs. Maharaja Krishnachandra would sometimes come to hear them in the Panchavati. As soon as Aju Gonsai knew of the Maharaja's arrival, he would hasten to the spot. As Ramprasad, lost in himself, went on singing song after song in the name of the Divine Mother, Aju Gonsai would at once compose doggerel verses in reply. As the Maharaja would appreciate his songs, scintillating wit and humour, Aju would get excited, elated and flushed, and make himself a regular nuisance to Ramprasad, who would often be in deepest spiritual moods. One day, out of sheer disgust, Ramprasad remarked that the effect of karma, the oiliness of a piece of wood soaked in oil, and the tendency to madness, do not leave one even after death. The reference to madness was a hit to Aju Gonsai. Pat came the retort from Aju Gonsai: One cannot get rid of the tie of karma, the habit of study, and the intoxication of wine even with death. 'Intoxication of wine' was aimed at Ramprasad, who, for his sadhana, would now and then take wine as required in the Tantric disciplines.

One or two examples of Aju Gonsai's performance will be found interesting. As mentioned above, one of Ramprasad's most inspiring songs was:

*Taking the name of Kali, dive deep down, O mind,
 Into the heart's fathomless depths,
 Where many a precious gem lies hid...

Aju Gonsai came out with a rejoinder:

Dive not, O mind, very often[14]
For your breath will get choked in no time.
You, a phlegmatic type,
        should not do excessive diving.
If you contact fever, mind,
You will have to go to the abode of death.

---

[14] ডুবিসনে মন ঘডি ঘডি।

Too much greed brings one to grief,
Why labour in vain?
O mind, dive not;
Just go floating and catch the boat
        of the feet of Shyama or Shyam.

Ramprasad sang:

*Come, let us go for a walk, O mind,
        to Kali, the Wish-fulfilling Tree,[15]
And there beneath It
        gather the four fruits of life…

Aju Gonsai's reply was:

Why, O mind, should you go for a walk?[16]
Don't you be induced by any one to go anywhere…
May be going to the Wish-fulfilling Tree,
You will pick a wrong fruit in place of the right one.

If Ramprasad exhorted his mind to behave like
a tutored bird, so that by repeating Mother Kali's
name, it could easily get at the Divine fruits, Aju
Gonsai counselled his mind not to be a tutored bird
for the good reason that none could possibly be
happy in imprisonment. He advised his mind to
understand that by repeating others' words one

---

[15] आय मन बेडाते जाबि।
[16] केन मन बेडाते जाबि।

could not know the Ultimate Truth. The fruit of mukti, he contended, grew on the tree of devotion. So he advised his mind to fly up freely and eat the fruit of liberation.

If Ramprasad sang:

This world is a mere framework of illusion.[17]

Aju Gonsai flashed:

*This very world is a mansion of mirth;[18]
Here I can eat, here drink and make merry...

It will thus be seen that though Aju Gonsai behaved mostly like a clown and excelled in parodying Ramprasad, he was not without some spiritual perspective. Unfortunately, only a few of his compositions are extant today.

---

[17] এ সংসার ধোঁকার টাটি।
[18] এ সংসার রসের কুটি।

# RAMPRASAD'S TANTRIC SADHANA

*T*hroughout his whole life Ramprasad practised the Tantric method of sadhana—a most misunderstood method of spiritual practice advocated in Hinduism—and attained the highest realization of Brahman. To understand the mind of Ramprasad, especially the meaning of his songs, we require to have some idea of his method of sadhana.

The ultimate Reality, called Brahman, the realization of which is the be-all and end-all of human life, cannot be comprehended except through Shakti, which creates, sustains and dissolves the universe. While Brahman cannot be worshipped, Shakti can be. Through worship of Shakti, the sadhaka comes to realize that ultimately Brahman and Shakti are identical just as fire and its burning power are identical. To come to this realization is the ultimate end of Tantric sadhana.

In a sense Tantric sadhana is Advaita in action. This Shakti could not be realized by man if it were not already present in him. What is in the macrocosm is also in the microcosm. This is how it is possible for man to realize the Adyashakti as his very being. The Shakti that is manifested in the universe lies in subtle, dormant form in every human being, and this is known as Kula-Kundalini. By rousing this Kula-Kundalini, according to prescribed methods, one can realize the identity between the Shakti, with which one's very own being is charged, and the Adyashakti Itself. And this Adyashakti is ultimately identical with Brahman. Through the practice of Tantric sadhana, Ramprasad attained the knowledge of Brahman, and thus proved the efficacy and truth of this scripture of the Hindus. After him, Sri Ramakrishna did the same.

Of all the modes of sadhana advocated in Hinduism, Tantric sadhana is the most positivistic and realistic in conception and practice. In this sadhana, the unregenerate human being of flesh and blood with innumerable desires is taken sympathetically from just where he stands. His desires are duly acknowledged and provided for in the scheme of sadhana, which is known as *pancha-makara*.[19] The idea is gradually to

---

[19] The five essentials of the left-hand Tantra ritual, of which the first letter is M., are *madya*, wine; *mamsa*, meat; *matsya*, fish; *mudra*, ritualistic intertwining of fingers, and *maithuna*, sexual union.

lift the sadhaka from the quagmire of desires to the pinnacle of renunciation, without doing undue violence to his sensibilities. It must not be forgotten that though, in a way, the judicious religious enjoyment of desires is provided for, the sadhaka has finally to transcend all desires and reach the state of desire-lessness, without attaining which there can be no realization of Brahman.

Man, whose gross being is composed of three gunas, passes through three stages of evolution in this sadhana, namely *pashu* (animal), *vira* (heroic) and *divya* (divine), corresponding to *tamas, rajas* and *sattva*. By awakening the Kundalini Shakti through sadhana, with the help of image worship, with the articles of *pancha-makara*, the sadhaka rises from *pashu-bhava* to *divya-bhava*. In Ramprasad's case we do not hear about his sadhana in *pashu-bhava*. It is said that for about eight to ten years Ramprasad did his sadhana in *vira-bhava* with the articles of *pancha-makara*. And through these practices he attained to the *divya-bhava*. In Sri Ramakrishna's life we find that the entire Tantric sadhana was done in the *divya-bhava*. However, the ultimate realizations of both through this sadhana were the same, namely, that Shakti and Brahman are essentially identical.

## SARVANI, THE IDEAL WIFE

*R*amprasad did not formally renounce the *grihastha ashrama*, the life of the householder. But he used to remain so deeply immersed in his sadhana that he would not be aware how things were going on with his family members. Once in a while, when he came home, the sight of their misfortune would afflict him, and sometime he would even resolve to do something about it. But as soon as he returned to his seat of sadhana, he would completely forget everything else. After his mother's death, it was the silent and rigorous part of Sarvani, Ramprasad's wife, to somehow make both ends meet at home. One does not know about the spiritual attainments of Sarvani. But as the *sahadharmini*, co-practitioner in religion, of her great husband, whom she tirelessly and unostentatiously served, herself always remaining in the background, Sarvani was a typical example of Hindu-wifehood which finds fulfilment in serving the husband and helping him become a saint.

# AT THE PASSING AWAY OF A FRIEND

*T*hough absolutely indifferent to the affairs of the world, Ramprasad was not insensitive to the value of the spiritual companionship which a devotee like Maharaja Krishnachandra would occasionally accord him at his Panchavati. We do not know anyone else who understood Ramprasad better than Maharaja Krishnachandra. It is not therefore strange that we find Ramprasad, who did not care for anything in the world except his Divine Mother Shyama, hurrying to the bedside of the Maharaja before the latter's passing away. It was indeed a blessed twilight of life in which Krishnachandra got this inspired son of Kali to pour exalted melodies in his ears just before passing away with the Mother's name on his lips.

But the death of Krishnachandra brought about a profound change in Ramprasad's life. After remaining in a sullen and grave mood for a few days, Ramprasad now began to be in an ever blissful state, completely forgetful of himself—now singing ecstatically, now

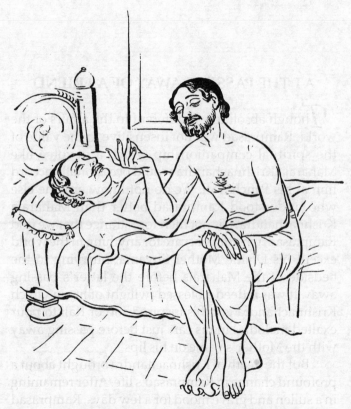

Ramprasad sings at the bedside of dying
Krishnachandra

mixing with all in unreserved joy, now embracing someone respectfully, now seriously discussing spiritual topics—and regarding everything with that equal vision about which our scriptures speak in glowing terms.

## SOARING IN SPIRITUAL HEIGHTS

*A* stage now came in Ramprasad's life, when sometimes he would be found dressed gaily, sometimes he would be found smeared with dirt and dust; and other times completely lost to outward consciousness he would be seated on his *siddhasana*, seat of perfection. Gradually, lapses in the normal routine of life became the rule of the day; food would not be taken and there would be no sleeping. Now he had reached a stage when it became very difficult for him to carry on the formal worship, for he was constantly experiencing the formless Mother within and without. And so he sang:

Oh, this is a hundred times as true as the Vedas—[20]
My Mother is formless.

_____
[20] ओरे शत शत सत्य वेद—तारा आमार निराकारा।

What then is the use of your making
                    images of metal, stone or clay?
Making an image out of the stuff of your mind
Install it on the lotus seat of the heart.

Even then, the lifelong worshipper in him would love to come back to the intimate, personal, sweet Divine Mother, who would be worshipped and sung to. Therefore, up to the last day of his life, in spite of himself, Ramprasad remained an image-worshipper, though he had long back transcended the necessity of ritualistic worship.

Such was the case with Sri Ramakrishna too. Even after being grounded in the experience of the reality of the formless Absolute, Sri Ramakrishna, like the homesick son coming from foreign lands, returned to Mother Kali with joy. His attitude in this regard is summed up in the witty remark that, he preferred tasting sugar to becoming sugar.

What is important here is to see that this attachment to the Mother, this returning to the starting-point after covering the full cycle of spiritual experience, does not connote any superiority of so-called idolatry, or a slipping back to the starting-point, but is an affirmation of the fact that Kali, to the enlightened, is the same as Brahman. When personalized, Brahman appeared to the enlightened one as Kali, and impersonalized Kali appeared as Brahman. Therefore, at this level of experience, when contradiction and contra-distinction between the personal and impersonal, the relative and the Absolute, melted away, return to Kali meant seeing Her always and everywhere, and at the same time seeing Brahman alone as existing.

# AFTER THE LAST DARK NIGHT OF LIGHTS

*It* was the lifelong practice of Ramprasad to worship the Divine Mother Kali with great éclat on the night of Deepavali.[21] For this great annual worship he would make the image with his own hands and be busy for days together collecting all the ingredients, with great care. People of the locality would eagerly await the coming of this day when they would find the great child of Kali worshipping his Divine Mother the whole night long with his characteristic fervour. Ordinary people could not understand all the extraordinary modes and nuances of this ecstatic worship. But they all found themselves inspired and uplifted by the touching songs which he would go on singing to Kali with whole-souled devotion.

---

[21] The festival of lights, also called Dewali, held on the night of new moon in Aswin (September-October).

The great soul leaves the body

A marked difference, however, was noticed in Ramprasad on the last occasion of the worship of Kali on Deepavali night. Unlike in previous years, he was not jovially greeting people who came to join the festival. He was lost to the world and completely wrapped in a divine aloofness which could not be disturbed by the coming and going of people. Seated in the worshipper's seat the whole night, he remained absorbed in the contemplation of Kali—sometimes piteously supplicating, sometimes singing without end one new song after another, spontaneously. Like one burning with leaping flames of Mother-hunger, Ramprasad passed that last great dark night[22] of life, transmitting warmth and light.

Next morning people found him as usual proceeding to the Ganga with the jar of sanctified water on his head all the time singing songs of the Mother, while devotees carried the image. Ramprasad slowly waded into neck-deep water and began to sing in his enchanting voice. One by one he sang four songs, the first lines of which will show that he was clearly aware of the coming end:

Wait a minute, O death…[23]
Tell me, brother, what happens to one after death…[24]

---

[22] Deepavali and Kali Puja fall on the new-moon night of Aswin.
[23] तिलेक दाडा ओरे शमन।
[24] बल देखि भाइ कि हय मरे।

My life is spent in vain...[25]
O Mother Divine, do you remember?...[26]

As he sang on and came to the last two lines of the fourth song:

Prasad says, the mind is firm by
    the power of Dakshina (Kalika);
O Mother, my time is out
    and I have offered my fee.

Ramprasad became immersed in Mother-consciousness and a light suffused his entire being. In that state of supreme ecstasy the great soul left his body through the aperture in the crown of the head (*brahmarandhra*). And the Bhagirathi (the Ganga) flowed on carrying his last melodious message in the casket of its own murmur to the ocean.

Of another melodious mystic, Sri Muthuswami Dikshitar (1770-1835) of South India, a junior contemporary of Ramprasad, a similar story of passing away is told. The incident took place on the night of Naraka Chaturdashi (the night preceding Deepavali) when Sri Muthuswami was singing a song in adoration of Goddess Meenakshi of Madurai with the words beginning *mina-locani pasha-vimocani*. As soon as he

---

[25] मरलाम भूतेर वेगार ख़ेटे।
[26] तारा! तोमार कि आर मने आछे।

uttered the phrase *pasha-vimochani*, which literally means 'the reliever from bondage', he was freed of the bondage of body.

This achievement of such unity with the Divine, that the soul and music of the mystic dissolve simultaneously and for ever in the music of the spheres, is a wonderful phenomenon, perhaps met with only in Indian mysticism.

# RAMPRASAD
## AS REVEALED BY HIS SONGS

*W*hat remains today of Ramprasad is the heritage of his songs, *bhajans* and *kirtans,* which constitute an undecaying spiritual treasure of the Bengali-speaking race. Just as Tyagaraja's *bhajans* move the hearts of hundreds and thousands of devotees in the South India, Tukaram's in the West, and Mira's in the North India, likewise, Ramprasad's songs enkindle the hearts of hundreds and thousands of devotees in Bengal. As long as there would be worshippers of Sri Rama, Vithoba and 'Nandadulala' in those parts of the country, Tyagaraja's, Tukaram's and Mira's songs would be sung; as long as Shakti-worship continues in Bengal, Ramprasad's songs will be sung.

Ramprasad's compositions may be broadly classi-fied into two categories: (a) the deliberate writings of a poet, and (b) the spontaneous outpourings of a sadhaka, a mystic; the former being *kavya*, and the latter having the character of *mantra*. To the first category belong compositions like *Kaviranjan Vidyasundara*, which Ramprasad deliberately wrote and presented to Maharaja Krishnachandra as a token of his gratitude for the latter's gift of a hundred bighas of land. Besides *Kaviranjan Vidyasundara*, *Shiva-Kirtan*, *Krishna-Kirtan* and *Kali-Kirtan* are ascribed to Ramprasad. But, of these, very little of *Shiva-Kirtan* and *Krishna-Kirtan* is available today. Ramprasad is specially cherished for and identified with his *Kali-Kirtan*.

The *kirtans* of Ramprasad are not just poetic words set to tune. They are, in fact, the yearning for and communion with the Divine Mother taking shape in words on the wings of tune. They are so to say the sound-forms of the Divine Mother Herself—*mantras* incarnating in the world through a suitable medium for the redemption of Shakti-worshippers. That these songs are instinct with the power of the presence of the Divine Mother is attested not only by the fact that they are so popular with the sadhakas who know the language of the songs, but also by the more significant fact that, like the name of Mother Kali, Ramprasad's songs were always on the lips of Sri Ramakrishna. On innumerable occasions, in deepest spiritual moods, Sri Ramakrishna found in Ramprasad's songs the most suitable medium for the ecstatic expression of his devotion. While singing those powerful songs, spontaneously rising to his feet and dancing in ecstasy, Sri Ramakrishna would often enter into deep samadhi. This is not an ordinary phenomenon. The songs of Ramprasad which Sri Ramakrishna would raise to his tongue and throw forth in rhythms of divine inebriation were not ordinary words, but the Mother Herself present in the form of the sound of those songs.

It was not in the ordinary deliberate way of a scribe that Ramprasad composed his *Kali-Kirtan*. But they came out of him with that spontaneity with which springs rush forth from the bowels of the earth. And they travelled from mouth to mouth and settled in the memories of devotees. Later on, perhaps, they were reduced to writing. It is not known with any certainty how many songs were actually composed by Ramprasad. 'I have appointed a lakh of lawyers,' this line in one of the songs need not necessarily mean that he composed a lakh of songs. At present there are on record about two hundred and fifty songs which are usually ascribed to Ramprasad. Even among those, a few are held to be compositions of some other 'Ramprasad'. There is a unique character of the soul in Ramprasad's songs which helps discerning sadhakas single them out from a multitude of like compositions.

Seated on his *panchamundi asana*, or standing neck-deep for oblations in the waters of the Ganga, Ramprasad would, as it were, be possessed by the Mother

Divine, and in the throes of overpowering absorption, would sing out song after song—rare, vibrant and vigorous articulations of flaming devotion—himself often fully dead to the outer world and only awake in the Mother. No one knows how many precious and marvellous outpourings of Ramprasad's soul were just wafted away without being recorded. As already mentioned, very often, attracted by his songs, boatmen would stop rowing their boats and people would assemble on the banks of the Ganga just to drink in the melodious rhapsodies of this singing mystic. They drank their fill and went on the way of their lives, perhaps even not knowing that the Mother Divine had vibrated into their inner being through the singing of Ramprasad. But oftener than not he would be alone with the Divine Mother in his Panchavati. Perhaps some of his most intimate and touching songs were sung to Her in this retreat, and probably as part of a dialogue, not as a monologue. It has been rightly said that genuine prayer is never a monologue; it is a dialogue. Most of Ramprasad's songs are direct, dynamic addresses to a very living person, the Mother, the child's only refuge.

In a variety of moods—supplicating or complaining, despondent or jubilant, cantankerous or humorous, thundering or adoring—Ramprasad brings before the Mother a refreshing variety of song offerings. Even as sea-waves of various shapes incessantly roll and break on the shore in unending importunities, Ramprasad's songs rush with might and main and dash themselves at the feet of the Mother with a reckless abandon—a power-play of amazing vigour and tenderness. Even while supplicating, Ramprasad evinces a power in his approach characteristic of the Tantrika *par excellence* that he was. A Tantrika does not know whining—he asserts his devotion, no mawkishness about it. His prayer is not a petition but a requisition, a pay-order; his absolute surrender is an all-out invasion. While he is ready to immolate himself totally in the search for the Mother, he loudly protests against the Mother's non-responsiveness. Ramprasad's was not the pursuance of a one-way traffic; the Mother too had to be son-conscious to prove the bona fides of Her motherhood.

Generally speaking, a chronological treatment of the compositions of the poet, philosopher, or mystic, who is being studied, is considered helpful in understanding his evolution of the soul. In case of Ramprasad, however, such a study becomes extremely difficult, if not impossible, because it does not seem possible to ascertain the dates of his compositions. But, supposing it were possible, one cannot be sure that it would be a dependable guide in discerning the evolution of his mystic soul; for the inward growth of a mystic does not seem to take place in a way that common sense can calculate. There are ever so many incomprehensible windings, lapses, undercurrents, bright moments, and glimpses. Even so, a study of Ramprasad's songs collectively, though un-helped by the compass or chronology, does not leave us totally un-rewarded. Through such a study it is possible to discern a soul-form—if such a term is permissible—of Ramprasad, chronology or no chronology; and this is what is important.

# RAMPRASAD
# THE MELODIOUS MYSTIC

*S*eeking to construct mood-wise the soul-form of Ramprasad, we find him at the outset in the mood of a sadhaka, a desperate seeker, pining for the vision of the Mother. He is convinced that the Mother is; there is never any doubt about that fundamental position. And therefore the agony is all the more acute.

In a frontal manner he asks the Mother a direct question:

> O Mother, how long would you make me go about
> Like the bull with blinkers on
> Round and round the oil-press?
> Tying me down to the trunk of this world
> You are incessantly making me go round and round.
>
> Due to what offence, may I ask,
> Have you made me a slave to the six oilmen?

Births countless of beasts and birds
      and so forth I have seen through,

Yet the cessation of this suffering is not in sight.
The word Mother is soaked in affection,
The way of the world is that
When the child weeps the Mother takes it on her lap.
Am I outside the world?
Countless sinners got delivered
By just chanting Durga, Durga, Durga;
O Mother, for just once,
      remove the blinkers from my eyes
So that I may behold Your fearless feet.
Wicked sons there are, ever so many,
      but never a wicked Mother.
(Keep Prasad, your wicked son, bent at your feet.)
O Mother, Ramprasad hopes to stay
      at Your feet in the end.

In a quarrelsome fashion he again chides the Mother saying,

It is not so easy as that to be a Mother.[27]
(One does not become a mother by just giving birth
to a child.)
To be a Mother one has to understand
      the anguish of the child's heart.

---

[27] মা হওয়া কি মুখের কথা।

Though he quarrels with the Mother, he knows where to hit and how to score a point. And so he cries:

Tell me Mother, where do I stand?
O Shankari, I have none to call my own in this world...

But a genuine sadhaka cannot all the time go on complaining against the supposed indifference of God, and imagining that he has finished all the spiritual practices and deserves the vision of the Divine. Ramprasad now rightly gives some home-thrusts to his own mind in a famous song:

*O mind, you do not know how to farm![28]
Fallow lies the field of your life.
If you had only worked it well,
How rich a harvest you might reap!
Hedge it about with Kali's name
If you would keep your harvest safe;
This is the stoutest hedge of all,
For Death himself cannot come near it.

Sooner or later will dawn the day
When you must forfeit your precious field;
Gather, O mind, what fruit you may.
Sow for your seed the holy name
Of God that your Guru has given to you,
Faithfully watering it with love;

---

[28] मन रे कृषि काज जानो ना।

And if you should find the task too hard,
Call upon Ramprasad for help.

The vision of the Mother is not attained without paying the price for it. Knowing this very well, Ramprasad, the earnest sadhaka, therefore piteously asks:

Will such a day ever dawn
When uttering the name of the Mother
Streams of tears will roll from my eyes?
When with the lotus of my heart blossomed,
Darkness of the mind will be dispelled,
And I shall roll on the ground
Uttering the name of the Mother?
With my renunciation of the sense of differentiation
All regrets of the mind will be gone.
Listen, as the Vedas are true a hundred times,
My Mother is formless.
Ramprasad declares: my Mother pervades everything,
O my blind eyes, behold the Mother,
Darkness enveloping darkness.

In a spirit of utter renunciation he subjects himself to severe self-criticism:

What is the use of this body, brother[29]
If it is not spent in the love of Mother Divine?

---

[29] এ শরীরে কাজ কি রে দক্ষিণাভাই প্রেমে না গেলে।

Fie upon this tongue
If it does not repeat the name of Kali;
Sinful do I call that eye
Which does not behold Kali's form.
That mind is surely wicked
Which is not drowned under the Mother's feet.
May thunder befall that ear
Which hearing the sweet name of the Mother,
Does not make one weep.
What is the use of those hands
Which only help to gorge the belly,
But do not bring the offering
Of Java, vilva-leaves and sandal paste?
Useless are those legs and they stroll in vain
If they do not happily carry one
To the place of Divine Mother's worship.
Can the Deity be under the control of one
Whose senses are not under his control?
Says Ramprasad, mango does
       not grow on the Babul tree.

But the greatest regret is that the dacoity in the sadhaka's life takes place under the very gaze of the Mother. Ramprasad, therefore, sings with a sore heart, and while singing, rightly gives the Mother Her due!

*Mother, this is the grief that sorely grieves my heart,[30]
   That even with Thee for Mother

---

[30] আমি ওই খেদে খেদ করি।

and though I am wide awake,
There should be robbery in my house.
Many and many a time I vow to call on Thee,
Yet when the time for prayer comes round,
    I have forgotten.
Now I see it is all Thy trick.

As Thou hast never given,
    so Thou receivest naught;
Am I to blame for this, O Mother?
    Hadst Thou but given,
Surely then Thou hadst received;
Out of Thine own gifts
    I should have given to Thee.
Glory and shame, bitter
    and sweet, are Thine alone;
This world is nothing but Thy play.
Then why, O Blissful One,
    dost Thou cause a rift in it?

Says Ramprasad: Thou hast
    bestowed on me this mind,
And with a knowing wink of Thine eye
Bidden it, at the same time,
    to go and enjoy the world.
And so I wander here
    forlorn through Thy creation,
Blasted, as it were,
    by someone's evil glance,

Taking the bitter for the sweet,
Taking the unreal for the Real.

In such a bleeding heart however blossoms the
bright lotus of a tender but invincible faith:

* I have surrendered my soul
        at the fearless feet of the Mother;[31]
Am I afraid of death any more?
Unto the tuft of hair on my head
Is tied the almighty *mantra*,
        Mother Kali's name.
My body I have sold in the
        market place of the world
And with it have bought Sri Durga's name.

Deep within my heart I have
        planted the name of Kali,
The Wish-fulfilling Tree of heaven;
When Yama, King of Death, appears,
To Him I shall open my heart
        and show it growing there.
I have cast out from me
        six unflagging foes;[32]
Ready am I to sail life's sea,
Crying, 'To Durga, victory!'

---

[31] अभय पदे प्राण सोपেচ্ছি।
[32] The six passions.

In an engaging manner, peculiarly his own, Ram-prasad tips his own mind as to how the vision of the Mother is to be attained:

*Come, let us go for a walk,
        O mind, to Kali, The Wish-fulfilling Tree,
And beneath it gather the four fruits of life.
Of your two wives, Dispassion and Worldliness,
Bring along Dispassion only, on your way to the Tree,
And ask her son Discrimination about the Truth.

When will you learn to lie,
        O mind, in the abode of Blessedness,
With Cleanliness and Defilement
        on either side of you?
Only when you have found the way
To keep wives contentedly under a single roof,
Will you behold the matchless form of Mother Shyama.

Ego and Ignorance, your parents,
        instantly banish from your sight,
And should Delusion seek to drag you to its hole,
Manfully cling to the pillar of Patience.
Tie to the post of Unconcern
        the goats of Vice and Virtue,
Killing them with the sword
        of Knowledge if they rebel.

With the children of Worldliness,
        your first wife, plead from a goodly distance,

And, if they will not listen,
        drown them in Wisdom's sea.
Says Ramprasad: If you do as I say,
You can submit a good account,
        O mind, to the King of Death,
And I shall be well pleased
        with you and call you my darling.

Even the humorous exterior of the song cannot hide from us the fact that herein are compressed the essentials of spiritual discipline, which one needs must undergo before the vision of the Mother can be attained. And one is convinced from the very accents of the song that Ramprasad was not merely theorizing but speaking from experience.

In certain states of his mind, the Tantric sadhaka can be amazingly fantastic in his approach to the Divine. Describing a comparable state of his own mind to Narendranath, Sri Ramakrishna once said:

Oh, what a state of mind I passed through! I would open my mouth, touching, as it were, heaven and the nether world with my jaws, and utter the word 'Ma'. I felt that I have had seized the Mother, like a fisherman dragging fish in his net. Let me recite a song.[33]

---

[33] 'M', *The Gospel of Sri Ramakrishna*, tr. Swami Nikhilananda, Chennai, Sri Ramakrishna Math, 1981, p. 564.

Saying this, Sri Ramakrishna sang this most bizarre song of Ramprasad which eloquently bespeaks the composer's strange state of mind:

> *This time I shall devour Thee
>> utterly, Mother Kali![34]
> For I was born under an evil star,
> And one so born becomes,
>> they say, the eater of his mother.
> Thou must devour me first,
>> or I myself shall eat Thee up;
> One or the other it must be.
>
> I shall besmear my hands
>> with black (Kali),[35] and with black my face;
> With black I shall besmear
>> the whole of my body.
> And when Death seizes me,
>> with black I shall besmear his face.
> O Mother, I shall eat Thee up but not digest Thee,
> I shall install Thee in my heart
> And make Thee offerings with my mind.
>
> You may say that by eating
>> Kali I shall embroil myself

---

[34] ए बार काली तोमाय ख़ाबो।

[35] There is pun in the word 'Kali'. It means Divine Mother and black ink. Apply 'Kali' on the face of Death may mean, defeating Death.

With Kala, Her Husband, but I am not afraid;
Braving His anger, I shall chant
   my Mother's name.
To show the world that
   Ramprasad is Kali's rightful son,
Come what may, I shall eat Thee up—
   Thee and Thy retinue—
Or lose my life attempting it.

What counts in sadhana is this stubborn resolve to prove the sadhaka's claim on God or lose life in attempting to do so. This do-or-die frame of mind is itself proof that the sadhaka is already possessed by the Divine. Those who can fully endorse the repulsive imagery used in the song, find themselves rewarded with added strength proceeding from the core of the song, as it were. The power inherent in Ramprasad's songs makes the singing of them a rewarding spiritual practice, which is widely resorted to in Bengal.

As the awareness of the Mother devours his mind, burnt pure in the fire of sadhana, Ramprasad speaks a different language giving clearer picture of the Divine Mother:

 *Is the Mother a simple woman,
   born as others are born?[36]

---

[36] शे की एमनि मेयेर मेये?

Only by chanting Her holy name
Does Shiva survive the deadly poison.

She It is who creates the worlds,
     She who preserves and destroys,
With a mere wink of Her wondrous eyes;
She holds the Universe in Her womb.

Seeking a shelter at Her feet,
     the gods themselves feel safe;
And Mahadeva, God of gods,
Lies prostrate beneath Her feet.

In *Sri Durga Saptashati* (V. 13), the Devas adore the Divine Mother with a significant eulogy:

We prostrate before Her who is at once most gentle and most terrible; we salute Her again and again.

The Mother is simultaneously most gentle and the most terrible.

In quite a good number of his songs which testify to Ramprasad's direct vision of Mother Kali, he portrays Her as simultaneously most strange, most terrible and most beautiful.

The embodiment of all Power, the nude Mother strides over the bloody battlefield, Her might making the earth tremble under Her feet. Her dishevelled tresses cover the sky. Her flaming eyes, blood-dripping sword and deafening laughter strike terror in the hearts of all souls. And what an adornment! A garland of decapitated human heads round her neck and a girdle of severed human hands round her waist! Inebriated, the Mother laughs a fearful laughter and is ready to gorge Her enormous stomach with anything available, a few elephants not making too big a gulp. But with all that she is radiant with an inconceivable beauty. Than her, nothing more terrible can be conceived, yet Her right hands are ever outstretched with the gifts of fearlessness and shelter. All contradictions meet in Her. She is not easily understood. But Ramprasad gives a hint how the strange Mother's wondrous ways may be to some extent understood:

> *Is Mother only Shiva's wife?
> To Her must needs bow down,[37]
> The all-destroying King of Death!
> Naked, She roams about the world,
> slaying Her demon foes,
> Or stands erect on Shiva's breast.
> Her feet upon Her husband's form!
> What a strange wife She makes!
> My Mother's play, declares Prasad,
> shatters all rules and laws:
> Strive hard for purity, O mind,
> And understand my Mother's ways.

---

[37] শে কী শুধু শিবের সতী।

It is only through purity of mind that the Mother's ways can be understood and not otherwise. All our so serious affairs in life are indeed Her fun. Ramprasad, in a philosophic mood, views them as Her sport:

*In the world's busy market place,
>O Shyama, Thou art flying kites;[38]
High up they soar on the wind of hope,
>held fast by maya's string.
Their frames are human skeletons,
>their sails of the three gunas made;
But all their curious workmanship
>is merely for ornament.
Upon the kite-strings Thou hast
>rubbed the manja-paste[39] of worldliness,
So as to make each straining strand
>all the more sharp and strong.
Out of a hundred thousand kites,
>at best but one or two break free;
And Thou dost laugh and clap Thy hands,
>O Mother, watching them!
On favouring winds, says Ramprasad,
>the kites set loose will speedily
Be borne away to the Infinite,
>across the sea of the world.

---

[38] श्यामा मा उडाछो घुडि।
[39] A glue of barley and powdered glass with which kite strings are given a sharp cutting edge.

But to see and enjoy the Mother's kite flying is not to understand the Mother. Ramprasad ridicules the aspirant who tries to understand the Mother:

> *Who is there that can understand
>           what Mother Kali is?[40]
> Even the six darshanas are
>           powerless to reveal Her.
> It is She, the scriptures say,
>           that is the Inner Self
> Of the yogi, who in Self discovers all his joys;
> She, that of Her own sweet will,
>           inhabits every living thing.
>
> The macrocosm and microcosm
>           rest in the Mother's womb;
> Now, do you see how vast it is?
>           In the Muladhara
> The yogi meditates on Her,
>           and in the Sahasrara:
> Who but Shiva has beheld
>           Her as She really is?
> Within the lotus wilderness
>           She sports beside Her Mate, the Swan.
>
> When man aspires to understand Her,
>           Ramprasad must smile;

---

[40] के जানेरে काली केमोन?

To think of knowing Her,
> he says, is quite as laughable
As to imagine one can swim
> across the boundless sea.
But while my mind has understood,
> alas! My heart has not;
Though but a dwarf, it still would
> strive to make a captive of the moon.

True, Ramprasad makes fun of the aspirant who seeks to understand the Mother. But the real fun is that Ramprasad himself has been not only all the time making the impossible attempt to catch the moon but has in some degree succeeded too; and that too, by the grace of the Mother!

So we find that with his growth in devotion, his conception of Kali also grows in comprehensiveness. He sees Kali sporting in the other forms of the Divine. In a rare song Ramprasad vividly narrates that it is Mother Kali who has become Rashbehari in Vrindavan. Dividing Her own form in two, in one half She has become Radha, in the other, Krishna; in one half She has taken the aspect of Prakriti, and in the other, that of Purusha. The naked one has now put on yellow apparel and Her dishevelled tresses have been transformed into the beautiful crest of the divine flute-player. She who had bewitched Lord Shiva by Her glance, has now captivated the maidens of Vraja. The lady who danced in a sea of blood now bathes in the waters of the Yamuna. It was indeed a great revelation to Ramprasad to discover the essential identity of Mahakali and Krishna, of Shyama and Shyam.[41]

Ramprasad, who has been ascending to higher and higher realizations, now finds himself face to face with the cosmic form of the Mother. A lifelong image-worshipper though he was, when the higher truth broke upon him, how readily he plunged into it! Addressing his own mind he sings:

> O mind, why can't you
>           get rid of your error?[42]
> You won't open your eyes
>           and see how Kali looks.
> You know and yet don't know, O mind,
> That these three worlds
>           constitute the Mother's image;
> What a shame it is to worship
>           Her in a clay image!
>
> Shame! that you want to bedeck
>           the Mother, with paltry ornaments
> Who has decorated the world
>           with countless gems and gold.
> Shame! that you want to feed
>           with rice and soaked gram, the Mother,

---

[41] Shyama, denotes the Divine Mother, Shyam means Sri Krishna.
[42] মন কেনো তোর ভ্রম গেলো না।

Who is feeding the entire
  creation with a variety of delicious fare.
Don't you know, the Mother
  is sustaining the world with great affection?
Then why are you wanting to sacrifice before
  the Mother, lambs, buffaloes and goats?

This vision of the cosmic form of the Mother
naturally brings about a profound change in the
worshipper's mind, with a consequent change in his
method of worship. When the Mother is seen
pervading everything, nothing is done which is not
worship of the Mother. Ramprasad sings of this state:

Listen, O mind, worship Kali
  In any fashion you like.[43]
Repeating every day the *Mantras* given
  by your Guru,
Let lying down be considered prostration,
  and sleeping, meditation on the Mother.

As you go about the city think that
  You are circumambulating Mother Shyama.
Whatever you hear by ear are all
  *Mantras* of the Mother.
Kali embodies fifty letters (of the alphabet),
  each letter giving rise to one name.

---

[43] ओरे मन बलि भज काली इच्छा हय जे आचारे।

Ramprasad is happy to proclaim that
      Brahmamayi pervades everything.
In eating, think you are giving oblations
      to the Mother.

The spiritual enlightenment indicated by this song is high enough an attainment for any sadhaka. But Ramprasad attained an even a higher state than which there is no higher. In the previous song we have seen the sadhaka's every act becoming worship. But Ramprasad, in the final spiritual leap, transcends the necessity of worship itself and sings in mellow tones of the mystic's ultimate triumph where duality is not, where liberation is indistinguishable from bondage, and righteousness from sin, where nothing more remains to be attained.

*Once for all, this time,
      I have thoroughly understood;[44]
From one who knows it well,
      I have learnt the secret of *bhava*.[45]
A man has come to me from a country
      where there is no night,
And now I cannot distinguish
      day from night any longer;

---

[44] ए बार आमि सार भेबेछि।
[45] Spiritual mood.

Rituals and devotions have
    all grown profitless for me.

My sleep is broken;
    how can I sleep any more?
For now I am wide awake
    in the sleeplessness of yoga.
O Divine Mother, made one with Thee
    in yoga-sleep at last,
My slumber I have lulled
    asleep for evermore.
I bow my head, says Prasad,
    before desire and liberation;
Knowing the secret that
    Kali is one with the highest Brahman,
I have discarded, once for all
    both righteousness and sin.

Such was Ramprasad and such were the songs, that by their inner fire it enabled him to melt down the universe and find it to be made of the Mother alone. And what a blazing testimony Ramprasad left behind him! Sri Ramakrishna, in the agonizing days of his frantic search after the Mother, and often after singing Ramprasad's songs with a yearning heart before the image Kali, would challengingly cry out from the depth of his soul:

You revealed yourself to Ramprasad, Mother; then why not to me? I don't want wealth, friends, relatives, pleasure and so on. Reveal yourself to me.[46]

And the Mother did reveal Herself to him.

Today we have Ramprasad's testimony reinforced by the life of Sri Ramakrishna. If the Mother is hidden from us, it is because we have not sufficiently pressed our claim and thrown ourselves wholeheartedly at Her feet.

---

[46] See *Sri Ramakrishna the Great Master* by Swami Saradananda, Chennai, Sri Ramakrishna Math, 1970, p. 139.

## ANOTHER BOOK BY THE SAME AUTHOR

### THE STORY OF MIRA'S LOVE

*M*ira is regarded as one of the greatest mystics of the world. She is a very special emanation of the soul of India. Born in the rugged surroundings of Rajasthan in the very heart of India, she exuded the most exalted love for God, the Beloved. Though born a princess, for the Beloved's sake she became the singing minstrel of that road which leads to the Divine abode. The moving outpourings of her heart in the garb of songs sung for and to God, have become the most cherished spiritual heritage of India.

The illustrative sketches drawn by Biswaranjan Chakraborty captures in a subtle manner the divine moods of Mira and imparts a vibrating quality of their own and enhances the efficaciousness of the writing.

The publisher will not be surprised if *The Story of Mira's Love* is discovered by the readers to be a cherishable little thing stimulating their own love for God.